THE CASE AGAINST
DAVID SUZUKI

An Unauthorized Biography

SHEILA GUNN REID

Printed in Canada

First Printing, 2018

ISBN Book: 978-0-9950168-2-8

ISBN eBook: 978-0-9950168-3-5

Rebel News Network Ltd.

PO Box 61056, Eglington/Dufferin PO,

Toronto Ontario, Canada M6E 5B2

TABLE OF CONTENTS

INTRODUCTION:

A NATIONAL SHAME, A UNIVERSITY'S SCANDAL

In a secretive vote behind closed doors, the University of Alberta decided to give David Suzuki an honorary degree.

It would be a questionable decision for any university – Suzuki isn't a scientist, or at least he hasn't practiced any real science in decades. He's not a champion of the University of Alberta, or of anything Albertan. He's not a role model for students, or scholarship.

He's a political propagandist, an environmental extremist, and a remarkably intolerant celebrity.

His personal habits – including treating young women as objects – make him a poor role model for today's graduates.

But most of all: David Suzuki just hates Alberta.

Or at least everything Alberta is trying to become.

To Suzuki, Alberta and its oil and gas economy, are the source of nothing but disaster and evil. Want proof? Listen to him go on about how Alberta is literally wiping animals from the earth.

"Witness the sage grouse in Alberta: almost 90 percent of its Canadian population died off between 1988 and 2006 because of habitat destruction caused mainly by oil and gas development. But the Alberta government refuses to curb economic growth and protect the areas it needs to survive and recover," wrote Suzuki just a few years ago.[1] Of course. What would such cruel, heartless moneygrubbers care for a poor little grouse? You can't sell a grouse. You can't fuel a car with a grouse. Everyone should know those Albertans care only for their dirty oil money.

But that's just not true. Suzuki could have been lying. Or maybe he just didn't have a clue. Neither excuse is pretty. See, the sage grouse is indeed an endangered species. But not just in Alberta. It's actually doing better in Alberta than in most places in North America. Its habitat has actually shrunk more dramatically in places without an oil business than it has in Alberta. There used to be sage grouse in British Columbia. And Kansas. Also Nebraska. And Oklahoma. There once were sage grouse in Arizona and New Mexico. They disappeared entirely from all those places. But there are still sage grouse in Alberta.

They're struggling there, too, of course. The sage grouse is obviously not a particularly hardy species. But in Alberta, government is actually working harder than most anywhere to help preserve the grouse. It's against the law to destroy sagebrushes and other habitats that the grouse require.[2] And there are laws prohibiting where certain structures can be built, including things as minor as fences, so as to not harm the grouse. So, actually, it's the opposite of what Suzuki says. It's not drill, baby, drill, and damn the birds. Economic development actually has been curbed in Alberta explicitly to help the sage grouse, and it's

1   David Suzuki, "Ontario's wildlife needs continued protection," The Georgia Straight, May 21, 2013, *https://www.straight.com/news/383791/david-suzuki-ontarios-wildlife-needs-continued-protection*.

2   Government of Canada, Emergency Order for the Protection of the Greater Sage-Grouse, November 18, 2013.

surviving in Alberta better than elsewhere. Blaming the greedy oil and gas industry is just Suzuki's way of propagandizing against Alberta. He wants people to think Albertans are awful. Because he thinks Albertans are awful.

And because he can raise money off it, for his multi-million dollar "charity."

Suzuki condemns Alberta as a "petrostate," a term that normally means an undemocratic tyranny, as in Iran or Saudi Arabia, where oil revenues ensure the survival of the regime and pay for its brutality.[3] He spreads the lie that government just "rubber stamps" any proposed oil development[4] — so the Alberta government is somehow both totalitarian and yet also completely toothless. Consistency isn't the point, obviously. The point is to smear Albertans as unenlightened worshipers of Mammon, with whatever slander he can come up with.

As he puts it, Alberta "oil has never been about 'ethics.' It has always been about money."[5] He sees no benefit to fossil fuels, despite the fact that they have literally saved millions, and probably billions of lives, by allowing us to more cheaply transport food, and water, and rescue people from disaster, and provide lifesaving medicines, and keep people warm in dangerous winter temperatures and cool in dangerous heat waves. He says the only reason anyone would want to burn oil

---

3   David Suzuki, Keynote speech to Green Party Sustainable Economics Conference, *https://www.youtube.com/watch?v=Kc6g-fxFyvo&feature=related.*

4   David Suzuki, "Beaver Lake Cree case reveals flaws in environmental review process," The Georgia Straight, Aug. 27, 2013, *https://www.straight.com/news/415171/david-suzuki-beaver-lake-cree-case-reveals-flaws-environmental-review-process.*

5   Faisal Moola and David Suzuki, "It will take more than rebranding to make tar sands oil 'ethical'," The Georgia Straight, Feb. 1, 2011, *https://www.straight.com/article-371055/vancouver/david-suzuki-it-will-take-more-rebranding-make-tar-sands-oil-ethical.*

is "So you could run around on a Sunday afternoon," all you people doing your silly errands and seeing your silly friends.[6]

Suzuki condemns Alberta's oil industry as evil. As a crime against humanity, like human slavery. "It is the same thing" as slavery, he told journalist Evan Solomon.[7] Alberta, he said, "sounds very much to me like the Southern states in the 19th century," with its self-interest and materialism and its utter immorality. "Who would say today that the economy should have come before slavery?"

And so, when Albertans suffer, Suzuki seizes the opportunity. When Fort McMurray was ravaged by fire in 2016, the Suzuki Foundation sent out a note implying that the oil industry based there was to blame — and that it was time to get serious about stopping fossil fuels to cool the climate. "For decades, climate scientists have predicted that global warming would cause extreme weather events like flooding and wildfires to increase in frequency and severity," went the press release.

But it wasn't a "weather event." It was a fire. And fires have been the natural cycle of forests before humans even showed up on the planet. As devastating as the fire was that swept through Fort McMurray, scientific evidence shows that in the pre-human era fires were many times larger, burned far more intensely, and burned for ages.[8] The difference today is that serious forest fires sometimes occur near human habitation, which is what happened in Fort McMurray.

Meanwhile, experts said there is nothing to connect Fort McMurray's fire to climate change — "one cannot rely at all on this event," as an indication of climate effects, said Yan Boulanger, a forest ecology

6   Monique Beaudin, "David Suzuki and Jeff Rubin form an unlikely alliance," Montreal Gazette, Nov. 4, 2012, *http://montrealgazette.com/news/local-news/david-suzuki-and-jeff-rubin-form-an-unlikely-alliance.*

7   Yael Berger, "David Suzuki compares oil sands industry to slavery," Maclean's, Nov. 24, 2015, *https://www.macleans.ca/politics/ottawa/david-suzuki-compares-oil-sands-industry-to-slavery/.*

8   Michael Balter, "Raging fires, high temps kept big dinosaurs out of North America for millions of years," Science, June 15, 2015, *http://www.sciencemag.org/news/2015/06/raging-fires-high-temps-kept-big-dinosaurs-out-north-america-millions-years.*

research scientist at Natural Resources Canada.[9] And even the UN's official global warming think tank, the Intergovernmental Panel on Climate Change, said wildfires "have not yet been positively attributed to anthropogenic climate change."

But that didn't stop the Suzuki ghouls from attributing it to carbon anyway, and calling for action against Alberta's oil industry. "Alberta had twice as many fires last year as its 25-year average ... with fires consuming greater areas," added the Suzuki Foundation's press release. And as people were losing their homes, their jobs, and everything they owned, while Fort McMurray literally burned, the Suzuki Foundation decided this was the time to call for more anti-oil policies: "It's also important for governments, industry and citizens to live up to the commitments of the 2015 Paris climate agreement and reduce the causes of extreme weather and its consequences."

With a bright red "donate" button on the corner of the press release website. Donate to Suzuki's projects – not to the wildfire victims.[10]

And when, just three years earlier, Calgarians were losing their homes to severe flooding, Suzuki was just as smug and malicious towards them. Suzuki has always had a special loathing for Calgary, probably because it's the hometown for all the greedy, grouse-killing oil capitalists and their twisted slave-owner mentality. He trashes Calgary as an "ecological disaster"[11] and says the city's development is "sickening"[12]— despite the fact that the U.S. and Canada Green City Index, put out by the

---

9   Terence Corcoran, "Experts won't blame Fort Mac's fire on climate change. Neither should we," Financial Post, May 25, 2016, *http://business.financialpost.com/ opinion/terence-corcoran-experts-wont-blame-fort-macs-fire-on-climate-change-and-neither-should-we.*

10   https://davidsuzuki.org/press/david-suzuki-foundation-statement-fort-mcmurray-wildfires/

11   Michelle Thompson, "Suzuki slams Calgary," Fort Saskatchewan Record, Sept. 26 2008.

12   Karry Taylor, "Finding common ground: David Suzuki and Jeff Rubin join forces," The Calgary Journal, March 19, 2013, *http://www.calgaryjournal.ca/ index.php/ourcity/calgarynews/1586-finding-common-ground-david-suzuki-and-jeff-rubin-join-forces0.*

Economist Intelligence Unit, ranked Calgary in the top 20 of all cities, and the fourth-best city in Canada.[13] (Yet, when Suzuki has come to speak in Calgary, he's been called out for moving around the city's relatively compact downtown in a huge, diesel-burning bus that he leaves running while he's making his stops.[14])

So given Suzuki's revulsion at the city's very existence, it's little surprise that when the floods hit, and began destroying people's lives and homes, he didn't waste an opportunity to seize on the misfortune. As with Fort McMurray, experts said there was no way to connect the floods directly to climate change. Rivers break their banks sometimes. Calgary, with two rivers running through it, the Bow and the Elbow, has never been immune. Heavy snow had accumulated in the mountains that winter. It was melting just as the spring was exceptionally rainy. Neither could be said to be signs of global warming. But Suzuki said it anyway — effectively blaming Calgarians for their own misfortune, just as he had blamed people in Fort McMurray for theirs.

"We heard it this week (that climate wasn't a factor) as communities in Calgary and Southern Alberta were evacuated in the face of extreme rainfall and rising floodwaters," Suzuki wrote.[15] But he wasn't buying it: "We know burning fossil fuels and pumping carbon dioxide and other heat-trapping greenhouse gases into the atmosphere causes the Earth's average surface temperatures to rise … which generates increased extreme weather-related events." Those floods, he said, were the result. And once again, he took the opportunity to say this was proof we needed to "wean ourselves off fossil fuels."

It takes a particular nastiness to turn to people in their time of crisis and desperation, whether in Fort McMurray or Calgary, and tell them it's their own fault. That it's their sins against the climate that have

13   U.S. and Canada Green City Index, *https://www.siemens.com/entry/cc/ features/greencityindex_international/all/en/pdf/report_northamerica_en.pdf.*

14   Cyril Doll, "The Tory-fication of Reform," Western Standard, April 23, 2007.

15   David Suzuki, "Is Alberta Flooding a Sign of Climate Change?" Huffington Post, June 21, 2013, *https://www.huffingtonpost.ca/david-suzuki/alberta-flood-climate-change_b_3480005.html.*

come back to hurt them. That they must repent by sacrificing their own economic well being – and by paying money to Suzuki, for the privilege of being scolded by him. But then, Suzuki isn't generally accused of being a nice guy.

He's famous for his wicked temper. He's stormed angrily out of radio interviews because the questions didn't make him feel flattered.[16] He's had scholarships pulled from universities because a professor didn't compliment his book lovingly enough.[17]

David Suzuki is not a nice man, and he is out to hurt Albertans most of all. But as you'll see, the worst thing about him is that he harms the rest of us to enrich himself. Far from being a scientist, he's actually working to undermine real science, putting the lives of innocent people at risk in the process. Far from being an icon of the academic and speech freedoms that the University of Alberta maintains it is celebrating by honouring him with a degree, Suzuki believes in silencing anyone who opposes certain points of view, his points of view, even by jailing them, if necessary.

And far from being a champion of our nation and its values, he tells the world that Canada is "racist."[18] He has been called out for creepy behaviour involving teenage girls. He has been caught fabricating scientific data and claims. He harbours prejudice attitudes towards immigrants. But he gets away with it because people think he's a well-meaning environmentalist.

But as it turns out, that's the biggest myth of all. David Suzuki isn't good for the environment. He certainly isn't good for Alberta. And, above all, he isn't good for Canada.

---

16   Lorrie Goldstein, "Suzuki even makes Liz May look good," Sun News, Feb. 27, 2013.

17   Lorrie Goldstein, "Suzuki ducks Sun queries, spurns freedom of speech," The London Free Press, March 1, 2013, *http://lfpress.com/2013/03/01/suzuki-ducks-sun-queries-spurns-freedom-of-speech/wcm/02e07a86-9080-463e-a122-7e3b87ceff87*.

18   Matt Prepost, "Paddle for the Peace" videos, July 13, 2015, Energeticcity. ca, *https://www.energeticcity.ca/2015/07/paddle-for-the-peace-david-suzuki-on-dams-ecology-and-the-relationship-between-humans-and-the-environment/*.

CHAPTER 1:

FREEDOM OF SPEECH AT THE UNIVERSITY OF ALBERTA

Inviting David Suzuki to speak at the U of A was a shocking blow to students, staff and alumni, many of whom publicly criticized the university for such poor judgment. But the university struck back, insisting their endorsement of Suzuki was an act of "freedom of speech" for dissenting views.

But the University of Alberta doesn't have much of a track record when it comes to standing up for "freedom of speech." Take the little student club called UAlberta Pro-Life.

In 2016, this student group wanted to set up a two-day anti-abortion information display on campus, with the usual visual displays that these things include, like ultrasound images of fetuses and graphic pictures of abortions.[19] That's not everyone's favourite kind of speech,

---

19   "University of Alberta's $17,500 security fee on pro-life event gags free speech: anti-abortion club," National Post, February 23, 2016, *http://nationalpost. com/news/canada/university-of-albertas-17500-security-fee-on-pro-life-event-gags-free-speech-anti-abortion-club*.

of course. But these were students who actually belonged to the U of A campus and they had opinions and ideas they wanted to express and they felt they had the right to do so.

The university didn't think so.

As is the favourite tactic of university administrators, the U of A brass told the pro-life group that it couldn't have its information display unless it paid for its own "security." Now, how much do you suppose it would cost to provide security for a table of pamphlets and posters for two days? Presumably a burly security guard stationed at the table would be enough to dissuade any troublemakers from trying anything funny. Maybe it's a unionized security guard; this is a university campus, after all. So while your average private guard-for-hire might make anywhere between $13 and $20 an hour, let's assume these U of A guards make as much as $25 an hour. With a couple of shifts, guarding the table for 10 hours a day, for two days, that's 10 times $25 times two days, so, that's $500. Heck, maybe let's even put a pair of guards there — one on each end of the table. That's awfully secure. The bill: $1,000.

Now, that's the kind of fee the school should cover anyway, out of the money those students and others pay to go there specifically so they can explore ideas and be exposed to other people's ideas. Protecting freedom of speech has a cost, sometimes, but the school can afford a few hundred bucks.

But the U of A wouldn't cover that fee. In fact, it didn't just ask the students for $500 or $1,000 to as a "security fee" to protect their very own supposed freedom of speech. Here's how much the school demanded:

$17,500.

Repeat: seventeen thousand, five hundred dollars.

To protect a table.

Staffed by its own students.

For two days.

The odds of a few religious students being able to raise that kind of money just to pay for an information table are obviously minuscule to begin with. But just to make sure there was virtually zero chance of it, the U of A gave them all of 11 days' notice. And it demanded the first $9,000 as an early deposit.

The school won. The kids cancelled. Their speech was silenced.

This didn't happen in some bygone era. This was in 2016, one year before the 2017–18 school year, which is when the U of A decided it would award its prestigious honour to Suzuki. An award that U of A president David Turpin defends because "Universities must not be afraid of controversy. Instead, we must be its champion."

Was the U of A championing controversy when it came up with an underhanded way to shut down that abortion display? Was it unafraid of controversy when it used a punitive fee to ensure it wouldn't have to deal with a few students who might be offended by photographs? Did the U of A even muster the courage to tell people that if they didn't like the display they didn't have to look at it?

Like hell.

Turpin's explanations are absolute baloney. The defenders-of-freedom bit is just a gussied-up rationalization to justify plowing ahead with awarding a degree to one of the most vicious, duplicitous, hypocritical and determined enemies of Alberta, anywhere. Suzuki hasn't been an academic in decades. And this isn't about free speech.

Listen to Turpin, as he explains himself in a self-congratulatory op-ed he wrote in the *Calgary Sun*, and while you do, keep in mind the cowardly stunt this same administration pulled less than two years earlier to demolish the speech of a few religious kids who, agree with them or not, genuinely believed they were speaking out to protect human life[20]:

20   *http://calgarysun.com/opinion/columnists/david-turpin-suzuki-controversy-shows-u-of-a-champions-freedom-of-thought/wcm/77d6aee5-81fb-4d1a-b21f-320dcc48b2ae*

"We will stand by our decision because our reputation as a university — an institution founded on the principles of freedom of inquiry, academic integrity, and independence — depends on it," Turpin wrote. "Stifle controversy and you also stifle the pursuit of knowledge, the generation of ideas, and the discovery of new truths. Take uncomfortable ideas, debate, and conflict out of the university and its fundamental role in society disappears. There are few, if any, organizations in society that can tolerate the discord that comes along with freedom of inquiry. That is the university's special role. To preserve it, we must allow our people, and honour others, who pursue ideas that sometimes trouble us, shock our sense of the true and right, and even provoke our anger."

And yet he goes on. And on. "The university must give people the space and support they need to think independently without fear of external control or reprisal. Otherwise, the constraint on the imagination and the intelligence will slow the speed of change and innovation, if not suppress it altogether…." etc. etc. for hundreds of more words. Could it be he's overcompensating for something?

How much money has Turpin cost the U of A with this decision to bestow its highest honour on Suzuki? How much money will the U of A spend out of its students' fees and government funding to accommodate Suzuki, he who travels like a celebrity? And how much public money will it spend for security on Suzuki's visit, despite the fact that he doesn't even attend the school?

You can be sure that even if it's $17,500, they won't be sticking Suzuki with the tab.

No one should buy Turpin's bull. This has nothing at all to do with academic freedom. Not even a little bit. It never did. How could it? Suzuki hasn't published scientific research in ages. He has no role at the U of A. And what's more, he literally enjoys an exponentially larger platform than nearly every other Canadian alive, funded by taxpayers, at the country's largest national network, the CBC. That's in addition to having his very own foundation, the David Suzuki Foundation, and publishing newspaper columns across the country.

Suzuki is not giving a lecture; it's not a debate, where the other side of the argument will be made. Suzuki will not accept questions from students – he almost never accepts unvetted questions at his other public events; he almost never agrees to debates. There is nothing academic about this honour, other than it is being done in the name of a university, and that university graduates and their families are being forced to endure it.

Calling this a defence of academic freedom is actually Orwellian in how offensively it contradicts the reality. Like *Nineteen Eighty-Four's* Ministry of Truth, which peddled lies, the U of A's is claiming to protect the "academic freedom" of someone who hasn't published scientific research in decades, and who already has more freedom than anyone to push his ideas. If that weren't bizarre enough, Suzuki's positions are pretty much the opposite of controversial. He's a global warming believer who argues that we need to stop burning so much oil. Kind of like, um, the prime minister. And his cabinet. And the entire government bureaucracy everywhere from Ottawa to Toronto to Victoria. And every university faculty in the land, and the CBC, and the UN, and Hollywood, and the EU....

David Suzuki is a TV celebrity like Dr. Oz or Oprah and he's just as likely as they are to engage in junk science and pseudo-science and spiritual mysticism as they are. (He once tried apologizing to a river for humanity's sins of pollution.[21] Seriously. He spoke to a river. This is supposedly a man of "science"?). If the U of A is willing to so badly mutilate the meanings of such vital western ideas as "scientific freedom" and "freedom of speech" to defend awarding an honorary degree to a vain TV celebrity, then it could just as easily do it for someone like, say, Bill Cosby.

That's not a wild thought exercise, by the way. Bill Cosby, like Suzuki, was once upon a time showered with dozens of honorary degrees. But after Cosby was accused and then convicted of sexual assault, university after university began revoking those degrees: Ohio State,

21   David Warick, "'We can't go on this way': rally emphasizes waterway protection," Saskatoon Star-Phoenix, September 19, 2016, *http://thestarphoenix.com/news/local-news/we-cant-go-on-this-way-rally-emphasizes-waterway-protection*.

Johns Hopkins University, Temple University, Gettysburg College in Pennsylvania, the University of Cincinnati. Yale University even reversed its own policy of not revoking degrees just so it could revoke Cosby's.[22]

No one would have the nerve to suggest that a university reversing its decision to honour Bill Cosby is somehow a violation of the principles of academic freedom. Of course not. These universities never cared about Bill Cosby's academic freedom. They invited him to accept an award because he was a star. And they wanted their universities to be in Bill Cosby's orbit. They wanted to elevate their schools by hitching their convocation ceremonies to the huge celebrity status of Bill Cosby. Now that he's been disgraced, they want nothing to do with him. They're making the right call.

But they're also exposing the honorary degree racket for what it is right at the moment when the U of A really would rather they didn't. Honorary degrees are given as praise. They are seals of approval. As it says right there in their name, these are honours. They are not exercises in academia or freedom of speech. They count for nothing more than the reputation of the school and the person they're being awarded to.

The University of Alberta had made the unbelievable decision to honour David Suzuki — a man who has devoted decades now to putting an end to Alberta's oil and gas industry and attacking the livelihoods of the graduates of that school whose careers are directly affected by the industry. When Albertans grew outraged, the university's president hastily invented an excuse for ignoring their concerns, explaining in his most bombastic and superior tones that this was some vital stand for

---

22   Emily Shugerman, "Five universities revoke Bill Cosby's honorary degrees after sexual assault conviction," The Independent, April 28, 2018, *https://www. independent.co.uk/news/world/americas/bill-cosby-convicted-sexual-assault-honorary-degrees-revoked-temple-university-a8326491.html*; Dustin B. Levy, "Gettysburg College rescinds Bill Cosby's honorary degree," Evening Sun, May 7, 2018, *https:// www.eveningsun.com/story/news/2018/05/07/gettysburg-college-rescinds-bill-cosbys-honorary-degree/587327002/*; Maria Puente, "Bill Cosby: Yale yanks honorary degree, TV Academy reviews Hall of Fame status," May 2, 2018, https://www.usatoday. com/story/life/2018/05/02/yale-yanks-bill-cosbys-honorary-degree-after-sex-assault-conviction/572788002/.

academics and speech and freedom. But this is not about academics, there are no freedoms at stake here, and Turpin's university has proven that it's actually a cowardly institution when genuine, controversial freedom-of-speech issues are at stake.

And in the case of UAlberta Pro-Life. The number of examples in which the University of Alberta has not just refused to stand up for freedoms of speech and academics are actually pretty troubling. Just a few months after administrators revealed the lengths to which they would go to silence those pro-life kids, the school was at it again, launching a faculty investigation into a silly, satirical article in the student paper after the piece was called sexist. Eventually, the article was erased completely from the website.[23]

Then there was the time that professors from the medical school voted to cut off funding for one of the U of A's public health professors because he was investigating ways to make tobacco use safer for addicts, which ran against their fiercely anti-tobacco opinions.[24] When the researcher then tried to hold an event that was literally called the "Conference on Academic Freedom and Research Integrity," to stand up for those very things, they had that shut down, too, all while the U of A's administration stood by and watched.

And before that, there was the time the U of A unleashed an inquiry on a professor and pressured him to stop talking to the media because he upset local teachers and school boards by suggesting there was a crack cocaine epidemic in Edmonton's schools. He was eventually cleared, but for that one, the national non-profit Society for Academic Freedom and Scholarship was moved to speak out, calling the campaign against the professor "an abuse of process that is apt to have a severely chilling effect on campus free speech."

And there are even more examples. And just like the ones just mentioned, they all have the same thing in common. All are cases where the U of

---

23   Nola Keeler, "'Misogynist' article removed from U of A law school website," Nov. 25, 2016, *http://www.cbc.ca/news/canada/edmonton/misogynist-article-removed-from-u-of-a-law-school-website-1.3868434.*

24   Kevin Libin, "Whither the campus radical?" National Post, Sept. 28, 2007.

A was entirely fine silencing free speech, squashing academic freedom and even condoning the harassment of professors, when the ideas, opinions and research were controversial because they were unpopular or politically incorrect. Being anti-abortion isn't politically correct. Trying to help nicotine addicts by making tobacco safer isn't, either. Neither is satire that might be offensive to some people. When speech is the least bit renegade and controversial, the U of A has shown it isn't ready at all to stand up for freedoms. On the contrary, it is happy to silence and squelch anyone who isn't sufficiently progressive and politically correct.

And that's why the U of A is willing to stick by its decision to honour David Suzuki in a way it never would for truly controversial people. Suzuki isn't a renegade. He's the opposite. His idea that we're warming the climate with our oil, so we need to live using only solar power, windmills and bicycles, would be at home not just in every faculty lounge in the land, but in every undergraduate student lounge, too. As *National Post* columnist Rex Murphy pointed out, "An honorary degree to a global-warming gospeller has all the controversy of a Boy Scout merit badge."[25] If the U of A actually did have any real guts, he points out, it would instead honour a skeptic, like Nobel Prize winner Freeman Dyson, who has withstood the slanders of everyone from activists to his own peers in defending actual, legitimate science against the claimed "consensus" of the global warming conformity. The U of A wouldn't be endorsing Dyson's heresy, of course. It wouldn't have to. It would be, rather, standing up for academic ideals. Or, as the U of A's president Turpin puts it so pompously, "There are few, if any, organizations in society that can tolerate the discord that comes along with freedom of inquiry." For universities to preserve it "we must allow our people, and honour others, who pursue ideas that sometimes trouble us, shock our sense of the true and right, and even provoke our anger."

But really, does anyone think the U of A would ever actually honour a global warming skeptic? You can be sure not even Turpin believes his own words about that.

---

25   Rex Murphy, "Dishonouring Alberta," National Post, May 5, 2018.

David Suzuki already has 25 honorary degrees. He doesn't need the U of A's degree to prove anything. For him, it's just another opportunity to hear himself complimented and show off another piece of sheepskin. And so it doesn't prove anything. Except this: That the University of Alberta's administrators won't fight for actual academic freedom and free speech, but they will fight tirelessly, no matter how much it impoverishes the school and its future for students, to rub David Suzuki's anti-oil, anti-Alberta ravings in the faces of average Albertans. And at a time when the province is still reeling from attacks on its product, its pricing and its pipelines from outside, the U of A is fiercely determined to help an enemy of the province attack Alberta from within.

CHAPTER 2:

HOW DAVID SUZUKI USES YOUNG WOMEN

The recent, powerful #MeToo wave of allegations of sexual misconduct against men of power has exposed more than just a bunch of creepy, abusive older males. It has also revealed how these miscreants were enabled by the people and institutions that protected their predations because they happened to be famous. And, in some cases, because they also were too important to some left-wing crusade or political cause. Just look at the shocking allegations finally exposed against Eric Schneiderman, the New York Attorney General and superstar of the American Democrats. In May 2018, former girlfriends finally exposed his violence and abuse in an explosive report in *The New Yorker*.[26] One of them, a dark-skinned woman born in Sri Lanka, told the New Yorker that Schneiderman, the paragon of progressiveness, this left-wing beacon of tolerance, called her his "brown slave" and demanded she concede she was his "property." But he kept beating and

---

26   Jane Mayer and Ronan Farrow, "Four Women Accuse New York's Attorney General of Physical Abuse," The New Yorker, May 7, 2018.

abusing women because, well, as the *New Yorker* reported, when women tried going public, the cult of political personality that surrounded Schneiderman silenced them. He was "too valuable a politician for the Democrats to lose," she was told.

When New York's Pace University law school awarded Schneiderman with an honorary degree a few years ago, it celebrated him as a hero to minorities and the marginalized.[27] "Eric has taken on the tough fights to protect New Yorkers — because he believes there has to be one set of rules for everyone, no matter how rich or powerful... Eric knows that the deck is stacked against everyday New Yorkers who work hard and play by the rules. That's why he locked up corrupt politicians who ripped off taxpayers, prosecuted companies that gouged victims of hurricane Sandy, and took on the big banks that led us into recession.... He's worked to provide relief for families hit hard by the housing crisis ... Eric has fought for justice for all workers, defending their right to a fair and decent wage for a full day's work..." and on it goes about how he is, well, let's just say, too valuable a politician for the Democrats to lose.

(Schneiderman also was invited to Pace to speak about — surprise, surprise! — his left-wing crusade to fight climate change.[28])

Pace University fell for the story that protected Schneiderman and his monstrous behaviour. But worse than that, the administrators helped enable it by endorsing Schneiderman. By signing on to his celebrity campaign they helped to fuel it, too. They wanted to glamourize Eric Schneiderman because then they could elevate themselves by bringing him to campus, putting him on a dais, and having him say nice things about them and their school.

---

27   Pace University, Elizabeth Haub School of Law, Honorary Degree Recipients: "Eric Schneiderman," *https://law.pace.edu/commencement/honorary-degree-recipients/eric-schneiderman/*.

28   Pace University, "News Item," Sept. 4, 2014, *http://www.pace.edu/news-release/%E2%80%9Cbeyond-gridlock-state-leadership-on-energy-environmental-issues%E2%80%9D-nys-attorney-general*; Pace University, "Beyond Gridlock (NYC)," The Pulse, *https://www.pace.edu/mypace/beyond-gridlock-nyc?mpc=cs*.

How much do you expect Pace University regrets that now? How much damage will this celebrity crush by Pace's faculty members cause to this school and its students, now that Schneiderman has been exposed for what he really is? How long do you think it will be before they have to rescind his honorary degree just to preserve a shred of face?

Universities across America are stripping Bill Cosby of his honorary degrees, but it no longer takes a criminal conviction like Cosby's for universities to feel the shame of being associated with a #MeToo offender. Allegations are enough. Broadcaster Charlie Rose has been stripped of several honorary degrees after allegations of sexual misconduct. In February 2018, the University of Pennsylvania announced it was revoking the honorary degree it awarded in 2006 to Steve Wynn, the casino entrepreneur, after he was accused just days earlier by former employees of sexual misconduct.[29] That's how fast universities are reacting to mere allegations of sexual misbehaviour.

In 2013, something very strange came to light about David Suzuki. To be clear, it's not the same kind of thing that came to light about Eric Schneiderman. Or Bill Cosby. Or even Steve Wynn. But in the age of #MeToo, the U of A should be very worried about the similarities that do exist.

There is no denying the facts of the story. They were exposed in black and white in the original documents obtained by "Access to Information" requests. When David Suzuki was hired, at great cost, to speak at John Abbott College, a public junior college in Montreal, the 2012 event took a creepy turn.

David Suzuki was already getting paid $30,000 to give a talk at the college, a taxpayer-funded public institution. But that wasn't enough. He wanted the school to provide him with an entourage of young

---

29   Chris Isidore, "UPenn revokes honorary degrees for Steve Wynn, Bill Cosby," CNNMoney, Feb. 2, 2018, *http://money.cnn.com/2018/02/01/news/companies/university-pennsylvania-steve-wynn/index.html.*

women. And they were told to dress in ways that he would like, as was revealed in the primary documents uncovered by Sun News.[30]

"I am contacting you because we have learned, via Dr. Suzuki's assistant, that although the Dr. does not like to have bodyguards per se, he does not mind having a couple of ladies (females) that would act as body guards in order that he may travel from one venue to another without being accosted too many times along the way," is what a staffer in the dean's office of John Abbott College, wrote in an email to Jim Anderson, a department head at the college for police studies, and copied to others involved in planning Suzuki's visit, requesting his help in recruiting the girls.[31]

"Why females you ask?" went on Mary Milburn, from the dean's office. "Well, he is a male." She asked Anderson to suggest "2-3 female Police Tech [studies] students for the job."[32]

It's important to note here that John Abbott is not a "college" the way that the Royal Military College, the Vancouver Institute of Media Arts, or Nova Scotia Community College are colleges. It is what they call in Quebec a "Collège d'enseignement général et professionnel," or a CEGEP. In Quebec, high schools finish at grade 11, and students who intend to go further attend CEGEPs before moving on to university or actual colleges. So the girls who attend John Abbott College are generally somewhere between 17 and 19 years old. The girls in Jim Anderson's police studies department would have been teenagers.

That these young girls were being asked to escort Suzuki around campus because "he is a male" is particularly unsettling, especially given that he was at the time a 77-year-old male. It rather comes off like one of those creepy cult leaders that surround themselves with nubile female devotees to both feel young and virile, and to make a show of their alpha maleness. But, unfortunately, this was happening on a public

---

30   Ezra Levant, "Saint Suzuki's scandal," Jan. 28, 2013, *https://www.youtube.com/watch?v=ejE9v6eVm7g*.

31   Email from Mary Milburn to Jim Anderson, Sept. 19, 2012, 3:07 pm, *https://nofrakkingconsensus.files.wordpress.com/2013/01/img272.jpg*.

32   ibid.

college campus, with a powerful CBC celebrity, and it was being taken entirely seriously.

Because, a few weeks later, Milburn followed up with Anderson to see how the arrangements were coming for Dr. Suzuki's all-girl retinue. "Have you selected the female students to escort dr. [sic] Suzuki?" she wrote him in an email. And she then asked Anderson if she could check them out to make sure all was in order for Suzuki's satisfaction. "Do you think I could get a very brief meeting or see them at one of their classes?" she wrote.[33]

Then things got even weirder. Soon, specific requests apparently starting coming in from Suzuki's people about how exactly the girls from the police studies program should be dressed.

The director of the foundation that funds the college wrote an email to Milburn, reporting to her that now "Dr. Suzuki does not want the students in full gear really 'undercover' look as opposed to their police tech uniforms. I hope that is ok…"[34]

Then Anderson passed along instructions to an instructor from the department who was evidently helping him recruit the girls. He emailed him to ask ""Please be certain the women are 'nicely dressed,' we don't want them in evening gowns, but definitely NOT Police Tech uniforms."[35]

Now, when news of this story broke, the school and Suzuki both put up a vociferous defence of their behaviour. They insisted that despite all of these emails, none of this actually happened. John Abbott College issued a statement insisting "both male and female students escorted him [Suzuki] throughout a full day and evening of activities in order to facilitate his movements throughout our campus. Those

---

33   Email from Mary Milburn to Jim Anderson, Oct. 19, 2012, 12:30 PM, *https://nofrakkingconsensus.files.wordpress.com/2013/01/img269.jpg.*

34   Email from Suzanne Beaudin to Mary Milburn, Sept. 20, 2012, Email from Jim Anderson to Joe Sledge, Oct. 19, 2012, 12:30, *https://nofrakkingconsensus.com/wp-content/uploads/2013/01/img270.jpg.*

35   Email from Jim Anderson to Joe Sledge, Oct. 19, 2012, 12:30, *https://nofrakkingconsensus.files.wordpress.com/2013/01/img269.jpg.*

students, all of whom were chosen for their professionalism, were part of our Police Technology program. There was no rider in Dr. Suzuki's contract specifying the gender or dress code of those assisting him throughout the day." Suzuki later talked about it with *Maclean's* magazine.[36] Reporter Jonathon Gatehouse noted there was, in fact, a "shred of truth" to the story: "Presented with an offer from the college to use students from its police training course as security, his assistant wrote an email saying Suzuki preferred a more low-key approach, and noting that he regularly travels with a female assistant who clears a path through crowds by politely asking people to move aside." Amazingly, that's really all the explanation he provides. He blames the whole thing, predictably, on a conservative conspiracy to discredit him.

Suzuki's version is that he was merely offered teenage students as security and his assistant mentioned that he regularly travels with females and the rest unfolded from there somehow, all very innocently. But that highly simplified version of events is hard to square with the emails in black and white. Notice that he isn't even denying that he prefers female escorts to male. And he told *Maclean's* he normally travels with an assistant, but his assistant herself told Mary Milburn that Suzuki "does not mind having a couple of ladies" around him. And every time in every email it is emphasized that it's females being discussed, which makes the college's claim that this was not about females seem hard to figure out, as well. And what about the fact that Suzuki was even involved in picking their outfits? And that they had to be "nicely dressed"?

John Abbott College never really owned up to its role in the Suzuki affair. It's been five years since those emails were exposed and then quickly dismissed by both the college and Suzuki. In 2018, would it be so easy to dismiss the casual joking about how Suzuki wanted young girls because "he is a male"? That they should dress a certain way? That they were talking about teenage girls as if they were an accessory to a septuagenarian celebrity? Not a single email shows anyone saying that this is wrong. That it's sexist or creepy. That these teenage students

---

36   Jonathon Gatehouse, "The nature of David Suzuki," Maclean's, Nov. 18, 2013, *http://www.macleans.ca/society/life/the-nature-of-david-suzuki/.*

are not arm candy for aging CBC celebrities. They all played along. They hopped right to it. They started recruiting girls. They screened them. They told them how to dress. At one point, the academic dean of the school, Eric Schmedt, even wrote an email referring to women as "darling Suzukiettes."

These are the kinds of things that should not be ignored. David Suzuki talks a lot about sex, after all. "Sex has been a driving force in my life," he wrote in his 2006 autobiography. "Only as age has brought relief from the high titer of sex hormones have I been freed of thinking of sex once a minute. Now it's about every five minutes."[37] In 2012, he explained that his "testosterone levels are dropping so people know that I am not after more sex…"[38] and has written that he's "delighted to see the role sex plays in the lives of Tara [my wife] and my daughters."[39]

People who have interacted with Suzuki's circle of protectors have said before they sense something creepy afoot. As columnist Jonathan Kay wrote in the *National Post* "I have had some dealings with the people who surround David Suzuki, and have found their treatment of him somewhat cultish, with each of his pronouncements being treated like pearls of wisdom from a Chinese emperor. When you have so many people drinking your Kool-Aid, it's only a matter of time before you develop a sense of entitlement to match."

The University of Alberta has decided to ignore the disturbing evidence around David Suzuki. It has decided to drink the Kool-Aid. There are people there who have apparently decided to join the cult. They evidently think they will elevate themselves by bringing him to campus, putting him on a dais, and having him say nice things about them and their school.

---

37   David Suzuki, "David Suzuki: The Autobiography," Greystone Books (2006). p. 378.

38   Kris Sims, "Suzuki quit foundation over fed 'bullying'," Ottawa Sun, April 16, 2012, *http://ottawasun.com/2012/04/16/suzuki-quit-foundation-over-fed-bullying/wcm/90908908-68d3-4fed-bace-4e4fb117afa8.*

39   Suzuki, "David Suzuki: The Autobiography." p. 378.

"David Suzuki is coming, David Suzuki is coming!" was the headline that ran on the front page of John Abbott College's student newspaper, *The Bandersnatch*, when it was announced he was visit there. They thought, then, that he would elevate their school, too. Instead, he ended up luring them into a discussion about using teenage schoolgirls as his escort accessories and exposed them to national embarrassment.

CHAPTER 3:

DAVID SUZUKI'S QUESTIONABLE ETHICS

They officially celebrate "Equity, Diversity and Inclusion Week" at the University of Alberta every March, but unofficially it's pretty much "Equity, Diversity and Inclusion Week" at the U of A every week of the school year. As with most schools, the concept of "diversity" is being shoved into every discussion, every classroom, every faculty meeting, every event, every decision about campus design and every cafeteria menu plan. Faculties issue official "diversity and inclusivity" statements. They conduct diversity reports on their staff. The school has undertaken a campaign to diversify its international student body.[40] It's a big deal. As the organizers of EQI Week explain, "Diversity of identity, thought, and scholarship advances institutional excellence."[41]

---

40   Juris Graney, "University of Alberta looks to diversify international student base," Edmonton Journal, March 13, 2017, *http://edmontonjournal.com/news/local-news/university-of-alberta-looks-to-diversify-international-student-base.*

41   University of Alberta, "Equity, Diversity and Inclusion (EDI)," *https://www.ualberta.ca/faculty-and-staff/equity-diversity-inclusion.*

But David Suzuki isn't quite so big on diversity. Not everyone has to be, of course. Yes, it is a bit ironic that as a grandchild of immigrants, Suzuki would be vocally and proudly anti-immigrant, but that's not entirely unheard of. Significantly less common is his belief in jailing people merely for their diversity of beliefs, thoughts and ideas.

People have called David Suzuki out on this stuff before, but as with so many things, his defenders work hard to shut down anything that exposes the darker side of the CBC's odious old uncle. In 2013, then-federal immigration minister Jason Kenney called Suzuki's views about immigrants "extreme" and "xenophobic."[42] The executive director of Carleton University's Centre for International Migration and Settlement Studies said he found Suzuki's anti-immigration position "surprising."[43] The *Vancouver Sun*'s health reporter once had a real soft spot for Suzuki, but describes how she was left troubled by an interview with him, after realizing how fiercely he opposes immigrants.[44] The reporter, Pamela Fayerman, had recently lost her father and felt only gratitude to the compassionate and hardworking Filipino nurses and aides who helped her dad in his final days: "Thinking about all of this in the aftermath of my dad's death makes me recall a rather troubling interview I had late last fall with the environmentalist/media celebrity David Suzuki," she wrote. "His views on immigration pain me when I think about the contributions of citizens from other lands, not to mention my own family's immigration experience."

Fayerman is obviously pro-diversity. She thinks immigrants make Canada better and, just as importantly, Canada offers a better life to people who lack the hope for one in their home countries.

---

42   Postmedia News, "Jason Kenney slams 'xenophobic' David Suzuki after environmentalist claims Canada is 'full'," National Post, July 11, 2013, *http://nationalpost.com/news/politics/jason-kenney-slams-xenophobic-david-suzuki-after-environmentalist-claims-canada-is-full.*

43   ibid.

44   Pamela Fayerman, "David Suzuki's anti-immigration views; an ode to the gifts of Filipino immigrants," Vancouver Sun blog, Feb. 18, 2014, *http://vancouversun.com/news/staff-blogs/david-suzukis-anti-immigration-views-an-ode-to-the-gifts-of-filipino-immigrants.*

But Suzuki doesn't care. "Is this what you're telling me? That it's a big country with lots of room?" he demanded of Fayerman. "We have this idea we're a vast country. But the reality is that a lot of it, a huge amount, is uninhabitable."

Suzuki wants to close the door to immigrants. He has repeatedly called our immigration policies "disgusting" – precisely because he thinks we attract highly skilled people. He'd rather that they stay where they are to work in their countries. He says we "plunder" other countries of their talent.[45]

Of course the reality is that people in those countries want to come here, to give their families a chance at all the blessings that Suzuki gets to enjoy. He says "Canada is full." But the man himself has five children. What he really means by that, plainly, is that he thinks it's full enough of a certain type of person. Surprising stuff for the darling of the CBC, a state broadcaster committed to unlimited, open borders migration.

But Suzuki doesn't just want to build a wall to keep foreigners out. He also wants to cut off our trade with them, so they'll be poorer, too, just for good measure. "We let Guatemalans grow our bananas, we let Hawaiians grow our pineapples … We use other people's land to grow things that what we need," he complains[46] (even though "Hawaiians" are American. It would be easy to chalk up Suzuki's views that trade with foreigners is bad as nothing more than far-left anti-globalization campus radicalism. But taken in combination with his belief that Canada's immigration policy is "disgusting," it's fair to ask Suzuki if he considers himself "alt right".

Suzuki's authoritarian streak goes well beyond who he thinks should be allowed into Canada. He's also made it abundantly clear he is dead serious about locking up anyone who doesn't share his political point of view.

---

45   Jean-Michel Demetz, "David Suzuki: "Le réchauffement climatique rend le Canada vulnerable," L'Express, Jan. 7, 2013.

46   Fayerman, "David Suzuki's anti-immigration views."

The thing is, Suzuki often pretends that he's persecuted, that he's the one who will someday be locked up for his views. He even performed in a live courtroom drama event in Toronto in 2013 called "The Trial of Suzuki," where he was supposedly being prosecuted for his "carbon manifesto" and its supposedly "seditious libel." Really. As the play's program read: "Will Suzuki's *Carbon Manifesto* save Canada or destroy it? Is he talking reason or treason? Is Suzuki undermining the financial security of the country? Or does the economy and country matter when our planet is turning toxic?" What drama. What hyperbole. What a self-appointed martyr.

When the Harper Conservatives were in power, Suzuki made the ludicrous claim to an Australian interviewer that green activists like him were in the crosshairs of a power-mad, environmentally destructive federal government. "We now have a government that is increasing the number of prisons at a time when the rate of crime has been dropping steadily over the last 10 years," said Suzuki. "So I'm wondering, I'm not a guy that thinks about conspiracies, but I'm wondering whether our prime minister thinks he's going to be creating new categories of crime, like eco-terrorism."[47] The Australian interviewer was sensible enough to point out to Suzuki that it actually sounded very much like Suzuki does spend time thinking about conspiracies, since he managed to come up with this wild idea that the government was hurrying to build prison cells just to house all the criminals it would be making of innocent people with laws that didn't exist yet.

Suzuki further proved his belief in bizarre conspiracy theories when he claimed that the Harper government's proposed anti-terrorism law, Bill C-51, would target Suzuki himself. "C-51 is going to put me in a category of being a traitor or an enemy of Canada," Suzuki told a 2015

---

47   "Saint Suzuki's toxic emissions," The Toronto Sun, Sept. 27, 2013, *http://torontosun.com/2013/09/27/saint-suzukis-toxic-emissions/wcm/2321639d-8902-4fd8-8f2e-1eb8dfb1cd3a.*

rally in Toronto.[48] The bill was passed, with bipartisan support. Yet, amazingly, Suzuki is still walking the streets.

Suzuki was obviously projecting. After all, no Canadian government has ever threatened to lock him up or even floated the idea of locking up dissidents – at least not since Pierre Trudeau's War Measures Act. But Suzuki thinks the idea of jailing people for their opinions is actually a terrific plan, as long as he's the one who gets to decide which thoughts and ideas should be criminalized. "I really believe that people like the former Prime Minister of Canada should be thrown in jail for wilful blindness," he said in 2016[49] referring to, yes, Stephen Harper, the same prime minister who Suzuki insisted was secretly planning to round up Suzuki and his ilk for "eco-terrorism" and treason. "To have a Prime Minister who for nine years wouldn't even let the term 'climate change' pass his lips! If that isn't wilful blindness, then I don't know what is." (Of course Suzuki was the one wilfully lying: as any basic search will turn up, Harper did say the words "climate change" — countless times).

Suzuki repeatedly calls for locking people up. A decade ago, addressing business students at McGill University, he talked about imprisoning politicians who are climate-change skeptics, or who were even simply unwilling to destroy the economy to save on some emissions. The students should "put a lot of effort into trying to see whether there's a legal way of throwing our so-called leaders into jail because what they're doing is a criminal act," he said. "It's an intergenerational crime in the face of all the knowledge and science from over 20 years."[50] "Our politicians should be thrown in the slammer for willful blindness," he

---

48   Fram Dinshaw, "McKibben and Klein lead thousands at Toronto's March for Jobs, Justice and Climate," National Observer, July 6, 2015, *https://www. nationalobserver.com/2015/07/06/news/mckibben-and-klein-lead-thousands-torontos-march-jobs-justice-and-climate-video.*

49   Jesse Ferreras, "David Suzuki Says Harper Should Be Jailed Over His Climate Positions," Huffington Post, Feb. 3, 2016, *https://www.huffingtonpost. ca/2016/02/02/david-suzuki-stephen-harper-jailed-climate_n_9143278.html.*

50   Craig Offman, "Jail politicians who ignore climate science: Suzuki," National Post, Feb. 7, 2008.

told PBS's Bill Moyers.[51] And not just them. He then added corporate leaders to the list of Suzuki's public enemies. "I believe what Kinder Morgan and companies like it are doing is an intergenerational crime but there are no legal precedents to pursue criminal charges on that basis,"[52] he said, referring to the oil pipeline company.

And it wasn't long before Suzuki was coming up with yet more crimes to go after corporate leaders, and Harper, and Alberta's provincial politicians, and even Australia's prime minister — so many categories and people being added to his list of thought criminals it might warrant building new prisons across the country. First there was his plan to prosecute people for wilful blindness (which isn't actually a crime). Then he wanted to throw in "criminal negligence."

There are, he said in 2012, "a number" of ways he could think of to lock up climate enemies. "You can charge people who are at a scene, where someone is being murdered, and if you do not do anything to try to help that, you can be charged with criminal negligence."[53]

Then he was combining them: "It is criminal negligence through wilful blindness," he wrote in a 2013 op-ed. [54] Anything to make the charges stick and get those climate enemies locked up. Anything at all. "There ought to be a legal position on intergenerational crime. If you stand out for a role of leadership and ignore the science on climate change,

51   "David Suzuki: Time to Get Real on Climate Change," Truthout, May 13, 2014, *http://www.truth-out.org/news/item/23675-david-suzuki-time-to-get-real-on-climate-change.*

52   Andree Lau, "David Suzuki Writes Letter In Support Of Grandson Who Was Arrested At Kinder Morgan Protest," Huffington Post, Nov. 24, 2014, *https://www.huffingtonpost.ca/2014/11/23/david-suzuki-letter-tamo-campos_n_6206360.html.*

53   Maria Rotunda, "David Suzuki Discusses Rio+20, Economics and Survival," Earthprints-Step Lightly, June 26, 2012, *http://myearthprints.com/2012/06/26/david-suzuki-discusses-rio20-economics-and-survival/.*

54   David Suzuki, "Australian scientists should be up on the ramparts," Sept. 23, 2013, *http://theconversation.com/david-suzuki-australian-scientists-should-be-up-on-the-ramparts-18505.*

I think that's wilful blindness."[55] Someone can surely find that legal position, somehow. Or just make up a new crime to charge all these climate enemies with. Maybe call it "eco-terrorism."

The University of Alberta's excuse that it will honour Suzuki as a demonstration of its commitments to basic freedoms looks positively absurd given that they're honouring someone so ready to deny those freedoms to others. Suzuki would violate the basic civil liberties of people just because they disagree with him about global warming. He would lock them in prison. He would jail our elected leaders for enacting popular policies, violating our very democratic freedoms.

And he's against academic freedom, for that matter. He once cancelled two scholarships he had sponsored at Carleton University after a professor there had written a less than glowing review of a couple of Suzuki's books in the newspaper. And he was proud of it. "That money comes straight out of my pocket and I can make the choice to stop that whenever I want," Suzuki said. "If the faculty regards me so poorly, why should I continue to support it?"[56]

Of course, faculty at the University of Alberta, some of them quite senior, have regarded the idea of honouring Suzuki very poorly, too.[57] But then, unlike the scholarship Suzuki spitefully snatched

---

55   "David Suzuki says politicians should be charged over climate change," The Whig.com, Sept. 24, 2013, *http://www.thewhig.com/2013/09/24/david-suzuki-says-politicians-should-be-charged-over-climate-change*.

56   Lorrie Goldstein, "Suzuki ducks Sun queries, spurns freedom of speech," The London Free Press, March 1, 2013, *http://lfpress.com/2013/03/01/suzuki-ducks-sun-queries-spurns-freedom-of-speech/wcm/02e07a86-9080-463e-a122-7e3b87ceff87*.

57   Gordon Kent, "U of A dean posts scathing letter against granting honorary degree to David Suzuki," Edmonton Sun, April 23, 2018, *http://edmontonsun.com/news/local-news/furor-erupts-over-honorary-university-of-alberta-degree-for-environmentalist-david-suzuki/wcm/a48dff40-8470-4f9b-8023-65989fec2966*; "Message from Dean Doucet regarding UAlberta honorary degrees," April 24, 2018, *https://www.ualberta.ca/business/about/news/articles-and-press-releases/2018/april/message-from-dean-doucet-regarding-ualberta-honorary-degrees*.

away from university students, this honorary degree benefits himself, so it's little wonder he hasn't responded this time by boycotting this university.

CHAPTER 4:

THE "SCIENTIST" WHO JUST MAKES THINGS UP

There are seriously scientific people at the University of Alberta who take academic misconduct seriously. A couple of years ago, the renowned U of A virologist, Dr. Lorne Tyrrell, made headlines when he said he would quit the school's Integrative Health Institute after it started turning into a showcase for quackery, such as naturopathy, indigenous healing, and "holistic wellness."[58] Other professors turned their back on the institute. "Quackademics," is how one of them described the group.

The U of A president David Turpin is an esteemed scientist himself, known for his research into plant growth (although he last published an academic paper in 2014 about, curiously enough, how often university

58   Paula Simons, "'Quackademic' health research must have no place at University of Alberta," Edmonton Journal, June 7, 2016, *http://edmontonjournal. com/opinion/columnists/paula-simons-quackademic-health-research-must-have-no-place- at-university-of-alberta.*

presidents get fired these days compared to historic patterns[59]). But Turpin is one scientist evidently not bothered by quackery. Not when it's quackery promoted by David Suzuki.

David Suzuki used to be a scientist, but he hasn't published anything scientific — not a study, not a paper, not a report — in decades. That's because he stopped being a scientist when he became a TV star. Now he's an anti-scientist.

That's not just some insult. Suzuki wears his anti-scientism with pride. The post-science Suzuki doesn't put much weight on research, evidence and inquiry. He's about living in harmony with nature. In 2016, at an event in Saskatoon, he spoke to a river. "I apologize to you, river, for our thoughtlessness…for polluting you, great river, we are truly sorry," he said.[60] He's a shaman. A cult leader. A quackademic. And he's proud of it.

He baffles, angers and alarms actual scientists by spouting off pseudo-scientific quackery, using the CBC as his national platform, gulling Canadians who might think they're hearing actual science. In fact, Suzuki has said he's counted on his viewers being uninformed. "When I started doing those shows, Canadians were scientifically illiterate," he said recently. "I had hoped that by helping disseminate information people would get better about making the right decisions."[61] By "right" decisions, he means decisions he wants them to make.

It's politics, not scholarship.

---

59   David H. Turpin, Ludgard De Decker and Brendan Boyd, "Historical changes in the Canadian university presidency: An empirical analysis of changes in length of service and experience since 1840," December 12, 2014, *https://onlinelibrary. wiley.com/doi/full/10.1111/capa.12087.*

60   Jason Warick, "'We can't go on this way': rally emphasizes waterway protection," Saskatoon Star-Phoenix, Sept. 19, 2016, *http://thestarphoenix.com/news/ local-news/we-cant-go-on-this-way-rally-emphasizes-waterway-protection.*

61   Sam Bronski, "David Suzuki, climate science's caustic Dr Doom, rips into consumerism, hails China's green tech," March 20, 2017, *http://www.scmp. com/lifestyle/article/2079813/david-suzuki-climate-sciences-caustic-dr-doom-rips-consumerism-hails.*

And among his most dangerous attempts at anti-scientific indoctrination is his long-time effort to spread panic and fear about genetically modified foods. Suzuki is a zoologist who hasn't worked in a laboratory in decades, but he's dismissed the entire body of work around GMOs as "bad science" and said, "it's money that's driving it."[62] The actual science around GMOs is the opposite of what Suzuki scares CBC viewers with. As the U.S. Genetic Literacy Project diplomatically put it, "Despite his background in genetics, Suzuki's views on genetic engineering are not in line with the scientific consensus on their safety."[63]

Real scientists have been fighting to counter the misrepresentations and fearmongering spread far and wide by anti-GMO groups, notably Greenpeace. That's because not only have GMOs not been found the least bit dangerous, having undergone rigorous, relentless study — a National Academies of Sciences report reviewed more than 900 studies, and found that "no adverse health effects attributed to genetic engineering have been documented in the human population."[64] They have actually been proven — scientifically, that is — to save people's lives.

In 2016, 131 Nobel laureates published an open letter to the United Nations and world leaders urging them not to cede to Greenpeace's attempts to ban "Golden Rice," which is genetically modified to include Vitamin A. Vitamin A deficiency kills an estimated 670,000 children under the age of 5 in developing countries every year. Even more go blind. The rice, given away free to small farms in developing countries, has literally been saving countless young lives, but Suzuki is opposed to the stuff, no matter how many kids' lives it might be

62   CBC, The National, October 17, 2001, *http://www.cbc.ca/archives/entry/david-suzuki-speaks-out-against-genetically-modified-food*.

63   Genetic Literary Project, "David Suzuki: Canada's 'science guy' turned eccentric anti-GMO, chemical scaremonger?" January 25, 2018, *https://geneticliteracyproject.org/glp-facts/david-suzuki-canadas-science-guy-turned-eccentric-anti-gmo-chemical-scaremonger/*.

64   National Academy of Sciences, "Safety of Genetically Engineered Foods: Approaches to Assessing Unintended Health Effects" (Washington, D.C.: The National Academies Press, 2004), https://www.nap.edu/read/10977/chapter/2#8.

saving. He dismisses the whole thing as a way for GMO to counter a "public-relations problem."[65] That would be the public-relations problem created by deceptive anti-science fear mongers like Suzuki, who would rather see innocent children die than see the public accept the truth about GMOs.

As the Nobel laureates wrote in their letter:[66]

"Scientific and regulatory agencies around the world have repeatedly and consistently found crops and foods improved through biotechnology to be as safe as, if not safer than those derived from any other method of production. There has never been a single confirmed case of a negative health outcome for humans or animals from their consumption. Their environmental impacts have been shown repeatedly to be less damaging to the environment, and a boon to global biodiversity. ... Opposition based on emotion and dogma contradicted by data must be stopped. How many poor people in the world must die before we consider this a 'crime against humanity'?"

But then, no one ever accused Suzuki about caring all that much about humanity. That's not an insult, either: He's proud of that, too. He's not just against food that can save lives; he's pretty much against the idea of mass producing enough food to feed a growing planet, denouncing pesticides, which have made modern agriculture possible, as the "dumbest thing" ever invented.[67]

That's because he doesn't believe we should have a growing planet. He's opposed to human growth and prosperity. He thinks humans are just another passing organism, no better than the rest, and usually much worse. When an actual scientist defended his own work creating genetically modified bananas to help further fight Vitamin

65   David Suzuki and Holly Dressel, *From Naked Ape to Superspecies* (Vancouver, B.C.: Greystone Books, 2004), p. 160.

66   Laureates Letter Supporting Precision Agriculture (GMOs), June 29, 2016, *http://supportprecisionagriculture.org/nobel-laureate-gmo-letter_rjr.html*.

67   Robert Arnason, "David Suzuki takes swipe at conventional agriculture," The Western Producer, Dec. 15, 2012, *https://www.producer.com/daily/david-suzuki-takes-swipe-at-conventional-agriculture/*.

A deficiencies in Africa, Suzuki scoffed at him. "What's the rush?" he said.[68] As in, who cares about a few more million people suffering and dying?

He's famously described humans as just larger versions of maggots that "defecate all over the environment."[69] He's also said humans are "like cancer cells."[70] We're "an invasive species."[71] He says Asian and African populations "are growing too fast" but "it's racist to say that."[72] Humans need to cull their numbers, he says, even if it takes a lethal "Spanish-flu-like" epidemic to wipe out billions of us.[73] "If you've ever been to Tokyo, you know human beings shouldn't live that way," he's decided. It's not often that you see a Japanese-Canadian expressing disgust at the Japanese.

Suzuki's certainly not that big on human rights, as his campaigns to ban immigration and lock up climate dissenters make clear. In fact, he thinks nature itself – animals, plants, and even inanimate objects like rocks – should enjoy the same rights as people do, enshrined in law. He's actively campaigned to have rights for nature written into our highest laws, the Constitution and its Charter of Rights and Freedoms.

"The benefits of constitutional protection of the environment are many and the drawbacks few,"[74] argues Suzuki, who was able to become an expert in these matters without ever having to attend a law school. After all, says Suzuki, "Our legal system is always evolving. Less than one

---

68   Miranda Devine, "David Suzuki drives me crazy," Daily Telegraph, Sept. 24, 2013, *https://www.dailytelegraph.com.au/news/opinion/david-suzuki-drives-me-crazy/news-story/c36584aad6c74697c43b95416d8e4ebc.*

69   YouTube, "1972 clip of David Suzuki comparing humans to maggots," *https://www.youtube.com/watch?v=LsLOcZQheoE&feature=youtu.be.*

70   Bronski, "David Suzuki."

71   ibid.

72   ibid.

73   ibid.

74   David Suzuki, "We can make Canada's environmental reality match its image," Dec. 3, 2013, *https://www.straight.com/news/541511/david-suzuki-we-can-make-canadas-environmental-reality-match-its-image.*

hundred years ago, women were not allowed to vote. Homosexuality was illegal …. aboriginal people couldn't vote until 1960." In other words, it's time we stopped merely apologizing to rivers and started telling them that they are just as worthy of rights as women, gays and aboriginals.[75]

Thinking rivers and rocks have rights isn't science. It's the very sort of primitive, irrational superstition that science — and universities — are supposed to reject. And by validating it, the University of Alberta is quite literally hurting science in much the same way that validating naturopathy and holistic wellness hurts medicine, as those university professors correctly recognized. The university's president, Turpin, has defended the degree as a way to honour Suzuki's "promotion of science literacy."[76] But, in reality, Suzuki does the opposite. He promotes illiteracy. He unapologetically rejects science if it doesn't fit into his belief system.

There is no shortage of examples of Suzuki just making up, apparently out of thin air, statistics and claims that he presents as "scientific fact," but are in fact quite opposite. They are outright lies. On a visit to Australia, he was called out for claiming in an opinion column using very scientific language that global warming was spelling doom for The Great Barrier Reef. He said a growing number of more intense cyclones could shrink the reef to a quarter of its size within the decade. Until a cyclone expert, Stewart Franks, an actual scientist, and expert reviewer for the UN's Intergovernmental Panel on Climate Change, confronted Suzuki with evidence that showed exactly the opposite. "In fact there has been a decline over the last 40 years and no increase in the severity." Suzuki's response? He admitted he had no idea.

75   "David Suzuki launches 'Blue Dot' tour hoping to alter Canada's constitution," Vancouver Observer, Sept. 19, 2014, *https://www.vancouverobserver.com/news/david-suzuki-launches-blue-dot-tour-hoping-alter-canadas-constitution.*

76   David Turpin, "'We will stand by our decision': U of A president presents case for honouring David Suzuki," Calgary Herald, April 24, 2018, *http://calgaryherald.com/opinion/columnists/david-turpin-suzuki-controversy-shows-u-of-a-champions-freedom-of-thought/wcm/d30289b7-b9df-4bcf-992e-ad4b3652739c.*

"I have to admit … All right. That was one, I have to admit, that was suggested to me by an Australian, and it is true. I mean, it may be a mistake, I don't know."[77] Someone told him? It may be a mistake? He doesn't know? He wrote these things on the public record as if they were fact, but they were merely a rumour, or a voice in his head. Or lies.

There's so many cases of this. When climate scientists found evidence that global warming was experiencing what they called a "hiatus" after 1998, even though they considered it a temporary blip in the longer-term trend, Suzuki simply dismissed the data as something ginned up by the "skeptic" community.[78] As if he had some special way to know the climate was warming, in his bones or something, that was better than the data from satellites and weather stations.

Suzuki fully admits he isn't interested in what actual scientists have to say when it complicates his narrative. "You know, if I say, well, the temperature range is blah, blah, blah … some guy will come up and say, 'I'm a penguin expert and I know the rectal temperature of penguins is not what you say', and we get caught up in those kind of generalizations."[79] But real scientists respond to data that challenges their hypotheses by getting to work trying to figure out what is actually going on. Suzuki, confronted with data that didn't fit with his superstitious beliefs, dismisses it as "generalizations" and just makes up his own version of things.

The list goes on. He makes up things about cancer, claiming that "up to 90 percent of cancer is caused by environmental factors" and links

77   Shaun Haney, "David Suzuki Gets Challenged By Actual Scientists in Australia," Real Agriculture, Sept. 26, 2013, *https://www.realagriculture.com/2013/09/ david-suzuki-gets-challenged-by-actual-scientists-in-australia/*.

78   Devine, "David Suzuki."

79   "Suzuki admits he got it wrong on cyclones, sort of, but please don't ask him about penguins," The Australian, Sept. 25, 2013, *https://www.theaustralian.com. au/opinion/cutandpaste/suzuki-admits-he-got-it-wrong-on-cyclones-sort-of-but-please- dont-ask-him-about-penguins/news-story/1a242d113032584d60064ba158ed6631?sv= 131d5405f8cfcec5ed82dd2d60cb53ba*.

it to the "massive use of pesticides, artificial fertilizers and literally tens of thousands of different molecules synthesized by chemists."[80] No scientific evidence suggests anything of the sort. The U.S. National Cancer Institute concludes, based on extensive review of scientific reporting, that somewhere between four and 19 per cent of cancers are caused by involuntary exposure to environmental factors. Only a small part of that is connected to pesticides and other man-made chemicals.[81]

And since Suzuki is against nuclear power, he makes up things about that, too, and makes it sound as if they're science. Like after the 2011 Fukushima incident, where an earthquake and tsunami damaged and flooded Japanese a nuclear facility. Suzuki capitalized on the tragedy, of course, and was caught just making things up to terrify people about nuclear power. He said there was a 95 per cent probability there would be another earthquake of similar size, capable of causing similar damage to other nuclear plants nearby. The radiation that one released, he said, would spell doom for hundreds of millions of people. It would be "bye-bye Japan and everybody on the West Coast of North America should evacuate."[82] He said he read it in a "paper." But it turns out no such paper existed.[83] The probability claim was entirely made up (it's been seven years and that earthquake still hasn't come). Scientific studies showed the Canadian West Coast actually suffered no adverse effects from the Fukushima disaster, anyway. And not a single death has been linked to the radiation released by the Fukushima meltdown

80   David Suzuki, "Biocentric Viewpoint Needed Now More Than Ever," EcoWatch, Jan. 24, 2017, *https://www.ecowatch.com/suzuki-biocentism-2203324815.html*.

81   National Cancer Institute, "Environmental Carcinogens and Cancer Risk," "*https://www.cancer.gov/about-cancer/causes-prevention/risk/substances/carcinogens*.

82   "David Suzuki Regrets Dire Fukushima Warning," Huffington Post, Jan. 20, 2014, *https://www.huffingtonpost.ca/2014/01/20/david-suzuki-fukushima-warning_n_4632950.html*.

83   Tristin Hopper, "David Suzuki 'regrets' claim that another Fukushima disaster would require mass evacuations in North America," National Post, Jan. 20, 2014, *http://nationalpost.com/news/canada/david-suzuki-regrets-claim-that-another-fukushima-disaster-would-require-mass-evacuations-in-north-america*.

(not even among workers that were at the site itself).[84] University of British Columbia nuclear physicist David Measday called Suzuki's scenario "ridiculous," "impossible," and "just crazy," adding, "I can't believe he would say that."[85]

But he should believe it. Because Suzuki will say anything that furthers his agenda, and leave people under the impression it's "science" by claiming he read it in a paper or has data points, when in reality his sources don't even exist. And he's admitted as much. He later explained that all the material he cited about Fukushima was "an off-the-cuff response" — despite having originally said he had read it all in a scientific paper.[86] In 2013, he admitted to the CBC "I have a lot of personal opinions, but that's not backed up by anything I know."[87] When the *Huffington Post* asked him in 2012 if and when he lies about stuff, he said "If I told you, then I couldn't get away with it, could I?"[88]

Maybe that sounds kind of funny. A little mischief. Until you remember that Suzuki presents himself as a scientist whenever he wants to fool people into believing whatever cultish ideology, whether it's terrifying them over nuclear power, discarding inconvenient data on global temperatures, deceiving people about the risks of genetically modified foods, or just making up fake cyclone threats to the Great Barrier Reef out of whole cloth. It's not funny, because David Suzuki does lie. Habitually. That's not promoting "scientific literacy." It's scientific vandalism. Real scientists wouldn't joke about "getting away" with making up data and research. But why shouldn't he joke about

---

84   James Concan, "The Fukushima Disaster Wasn't Disastrous Because Of The Radiation," Forbes, March 16, 2015, *https://www.forbes.com/sites/ jamesconca/2015/03/16/the-fukushima-disaster-wasnt-very-disastrous/#47180d346b2d.*

85   David P. Ball, "These Nuclear Physicists Think David Suzuki Is Exaggerating about Fukushima," Vice, Nov. 8, 2013, *https://www.vice.com/en_ca/ article/gq8gbm/these-nuclear-physicists-think-david-suzuki-is-exaggerating-about-fukushima.*

86   Hopper, "David Suzuki."

87   CBC Radio, April 18, 2013.

88   "11 Questions For David Suzuki," Huffington Post, Oct. 29, 2012, *https://www.huffingtonpost.ca/2012/10/29/11-questions-for-david-suzuki_n_1970736. html.*

it? He's not only getting away with it, he's being honoured for it by an esteemed university.

But the University of Alberta can't have it both ways. If David Turpin wants to pretend David Suzuki is an actual, serious scientist, despite so much evidence to the contrary, then he should be held to the same standards as a real scientist. And if you do that, then you have to acknowledge his fraud, his fabrications, his data manipulation and, based on his own admissions, what amounts to gross misconduct. That doesn't call for an honour. It calls for a disciplinary hearing.

CHAPTER 5:

ATTACKING INDUSTRY WHILE FILLING HIS POCKETS

If Canadians someday found out that, say, the country's most prominent and activist scientific expert on fighting smoking were actually being secretly funded by the tobacco companies, the fallout isn't hard to imagine. Obviously there would be something deeply corrupt about exploiting a professional platform to advise people about the harms of a product but not disclosing that you're benefiting personally from the very thing you claim is so harmful.

But what if it were the case that Canada's most prominent and activist "expert" on fighting fossil fuels is actually personally benefiting directly from fossil fuels? Not just in terms of how abundantly he enjoys using them personally —although, you would think that would be every bit as credibility-destroying as if an anti-tobacco activist were also an enthusiastic cigar aficionado. But what if he were literally taking money from the fossil fuel industry? What if he were making private investment deals with an oil company?

Because he is.

There are so many ways that Suzuki's personal interests are in direct and severe conflict with his public pronouncements and self-proclaimed expertise that it's clear his entire anti-oil act is really just that: An act. A deceitful and deeply corrupt act. And it's an act that does real harm. His activism to sabotage Canada's resource economy is nearly as cynical and cold as his efforts to prevent children in developing countries getting help for their diseases. He has cost people their jobs by agitating for protests and policies that stop projects that Canadian families depend on. He has cost shareholders, many of whom are Canadian pension funds that support retired teachers, nurses, and other workers, making life poorer for people who actually contribute to this country, while he lines his own pockets. He has robbed governments of the revenues from their natural resources, leaving them with less funding for hospitals, schools and social assistance for families in need. David Suzuki has made a racket out of harming Canadians so he can feather his personal nest. It's far worse than hypocrisy. It's a swindle. The rest of us get poorer so he can get richer. He's the Bernie Madoff of the anti-oil crusade.

Has he quietly been benefitting financially from the industry he claims he's fighting against? He most certainly has. Suzuki has long claimed that his foundation, the David Suzuki Foundation, is funded by grassroots support; none of that dirty corporate or government money. He also insists that the foundation's funds don't benefit him. As he told Toronto radio host John Oakley, "I'm not getting any money from my foundation. I'm getting my money, the foundation gets its money, from ordinary people. We don't take government money, corporations have not been interested in funding us. We get it from ordinary Canadians across the country, 40,000 of them, and we get some foundations in both Canada and the United States. So that's my agenda. We speak on behalf of the people that fund us."[89]

It's not an accident that right after he insists his money is different from the Suzuki Foundation's money he immediately goes back to

89   Joseph C. Ben-Ami, "Global warming charlatan," Institute for Canadian Values, Feb. 19, 2007, *https://web.archive.org/web/20071008023718/; http://www.canadianvalues.ca/commentary.aspx?aid=267.*

talking about it as if it's one and the same pot of money. "We don't take government money… We get it from ordinary Canadians …. we get some foundations… We speak on behalf of the people that fund us." When Suzuki was chairman of the foundation, he was slick enough to serve as a "volunteer," so he can get away with saying that he doesn't get money directly from the foundation. But his wife of 45 years, Tara Cullis, is president of the Suzuki Foundation and its co-founder.[90] And the Suzuki Foundation pays its executives a fair amount, according to Charity Intelligence Canada, which reports on the financial behaviour of charitable groups.[91] And Cullis isn't the only Suzuki family member working there. So does their daughter, Sarika Cullis-Suzuki.[92] Individual salaries are not reported, but a handful of people at the foundation that earned between $100,000 and $250,000 in fiscal 2016.[93] Remember, David Suzuki's wife is the president, and has been at the foundation since Day One — the two of them literally founded it together.

And about that claim that "we don't take government money [and] corporations have not been interested in funding us"? Another lie. And it's a lie he tells brazenly, specifically using it to buttress his fake credibility while shamelessly attacking others for accepting the same kind of funding he's been getting. In 2013, he told the *National Post,* "I would like to believe that Canadians also know that I haven't sold out, that is started taking money from corporations, so there is credibility in that."[94] But if that's his rule, then the opposite must be true: If he's been lying about corporate funding, then what's his credibility level then? Non-existent.

---

90   The David Suzuki Foundation, "About us," *https://davidsuzuki.org/about/ staff-board/our-board/.*

91   Charity Intelligence Canada, "David Suzuki Foundation," *https://www. charityintelligence.ca/charity-details/247-david-suzuki-foundation.*

92   Suzuki Foundation, "About us."

93   Charity Intelligence Canada, "David Suzuki Foundation."

94   Jonathan Kay, "Who would have thunk it? Angry Ezra is making media mincemeat of Saint Suzuki," National Post, Oct. 15, 2013, *http://nationalpost. com/opinion/jonathan-kay-who-would-have-thunk-it-angry-ezra-is-making-media-mincemeat-of-saint-suzuki.*

Because over the years, Suzuki and his foundation have taken funding from not just the government, through the federal Natural Sciences and Engineering Research Council of Canada,[95] despite claiming they take no public money. Their annual reports have also reported donations from fossil fuel companies like the Alberta natural gas company, ATCO, and the pension fund of Ontario Power Generation, which at the time was operating not only coal- and gas-fired power plants but has several nuclear power plants.

Suzuki campaigns against fossil fuels and nuclear power by day, while cashing the fossil fuel and nuclear power industries' cheques by night, and using the money to keep Suzuki family members employed. And Suzuki not only claims that it's all for charity, he benefits further from millions of dollars in government charitable subsidies for calling it that[96] — in other words, yet more of that government support that Suzuki acts like he isn't getting.

While Suzuki pretends that he's as pure as the driven snow, uncorrupted by any of that filthy corporate money, he slanders and smears as corrupt any group that offers a different point of view while receiving corporate funding. Suzuki attacked Willie Soon, a top researcher at the Harvard-Smithsonian Center for Astrophysics, because his research shows that most global warming is being caused by solar variation, and not emissions from fossil fuels, while having received some funding for his work from the American oil industry.

It wasn't that much money to begin with: US$1 million, which is just a fraction of the funding Suzuki's organization has pulled in over the years including from the fossil fuel and nuclear power industries, among other undisclosed funders. Unlike Suzuki, Soon hasn't lied about his funding: He disclosed in academic papers that he received

---

95   David Suzuki Foundation, "About us," archived Jan. 10, 2007, *https://web.archive.org/web/20070110063313/https://davidsuzuki.org/About_us/* FAQs.asp; Natural Sciences and Engineering Research Council of Canada, *http://www.nserc-crsng.gc.ca.*

96   Charity Intelligence Canada, "David Suzuki Foundation"; The Suzuki Foundation, "FAQs," *https://davidsuzuki.org/about/faqs/.*

private funding from petroleum interests.[97] And, also unlike Suzuki, Soon is a legitimate scientist, as he has pointed out, and cares only about objective evidence, not political activism or climate ideology. "No amount of money can influence what I have to say and write," Soon said.[98] To this day, he remains a researcher at the lab[99] — administrators have found no reason to dismiss him or his work. But Soon has noted that he relies on grants, not public money, and would be happy to let the green lobby pay for his research, instead of corporate funders, if it offered to.[100] It hasn't, of course.

And yet Suzuki, the phony scientist, says we should ignore Soon's research. "Let's stop wasting our time on deniers," he said of Soon.[101] In other words, disregard research from a lab connected to Harvard University and the Smithsonian Institute, two of the world's most prestigious institutions. But we're supposed to trust the activist, agenda-driven David Suzuki Foundation, which accepts money from not only corporations, but has received millions of dollars — many times more than Soon received — from mysterious foreign donors it hasn't even disclosed.

For years, the Suzuki Foundation underreported or simply failed to report any of its American donations. As investigative reporter Vivian Krause reported in the *Financial Post*, "In annual reports for 2001, 2002 and 2003, Suzuki's foundation mentions vaguely that it received grants from 'throughout North America,' but names of donor

---

97   Christopher Rowland, "Researcher helps sow climate-change doubt," The Boston Globe, Nov. 5, 2013, *https://www.bostonglobe.com/news/nation/2013/11/05/harvard-smithsonian-global-warming-skeptic-helps-feed-strategy-doubt-gridlock-congress/uHssYO1anoWSiLw0v1YcUJ/story.html.*

98   ibid.

99   Harvard-Smithsonian Center for Astrophysics, "HEA Staff List," *https://www.cfa.harvard.edu/contact/hea.*

100   John Vidal, "Climate sceptic Willie Soon received $1m from oil companies, papers show," The Guardian, June 17, 2011.

101   David Suzuki, "Let's stop wasting time on unscientific climate change deniers," The Georgia Straight, July 12, 2011, *https://www.straight.com/article-403433/vancouver/david-suzuki-lets-stop-wasting-time-unscientific-climate-change-deniers.*

foundations weren't given."[102] Yet, Krause was able to piece together through records that in those three years alone, the foundation hauled in US$3.6 million from unknown American sources, the equivalent of $5.5 million Canadian back then (more than $7 million in today's dollars). We have no idea where that money came from. Who knows how many oil and gas companies or nuclear companies were sending the Suzuki family business millions of dollars from the U.S.? And who knows how much it corrupted David Suzuki's public activism and statements as a result?

Did receiving donations from U.S. fossil fuel companies influence Suzuki's decision to attack Canadian fossil fuel companies – their competitors?

And what about Suzuki's personal deal with an oil company? He doesn't talk about it much, but this man of nature, who believes we humans are just another unexceptional organism, with no greater right to the earth than the maggots or the moss, is quite a real estate baron. He owns more of this blue planet than nearly anyone else on it. David Suzuki isn't among the one percent. He's up there with the 0.0001 per cent. He owns millions of dollars in property.

There's his main home, a "sprawling mansion" in Vancouver's high-end Kitsilano neighbourhood. [103] At $15 million,[104] it's valued higher than the homes of many Hollywood celebrities and rock stars.

He also owns a second house in the same tony neighbourhood, worth a cool million or two.[105] And a waterfront property on the coast of

---

102   Vivian Krause, "Suzuki's Funding," Financial Post, April 19, 2012, *http://business.financialpost.com/opinion/vivian-krause-suzukis-funding*.

103   Jessica Hume, "David Suzuki a man of property," Ottawa Sun, Oct. 10, 2013, *http://ottawasun.com/2013/10/10/david-suzuki-a-man-of-property/wcm/949b5f61-4d5f-4848-874d-1c738b18f821*.

104   City of Vancouver, "Vancouver Property Info Report," April 25, 2018.

105   Assessment Roll Report, 2018; Hume, "David Suzuki."

Quadra Island, worth another seven figures.[106] And a vacation home in Australia.[107] And … phew … still more.

Like this one: A partnership stake in a property on Quadra Island, co-owned with — get this — a company called Kootenay Oil Distributors.[108]

David Suzuki is literally making private business deals with a fossil-fuel company. There's probably no oil in the islands along B.C.'s Sunshine Coast. Who knows what kind of arrangement these two curious partners have made? Suzuki does, but he's not saying.[109] All he seems to have said publicly about it is that the company isn't in the oil-distribution business anymore. But he's evidently perfectly happy to use that oil money in his property deals nonetheless.

Suzuki will make a land deal with fossil-fuel money. He will talk about the need to abandon land ownership, calling for "rewilding" (abandoning our developed properties and letting them return to their natural state), while amassing a large personal private property portfolio.[110]

And of course, while telling us all that we need to stop driving, live smaller, have fewer children, and travel less, Suzuki has a massive family, with massive homes, and leaves a carbon footprint so many times larger than the rest of us. His co-workers say he insists on

---

106   ibid.

107   Michael Slezak, "David Suzuki: Australia's 'sickening' threat to marine reserves undermines global protection," The Guardian, Sept. 26, 2017, *https://www.theguardian.com/environment/2017/sep/27/david-suzuki-australia-sickening-threat-to-marine-reserves-undermines-global-protection.*

108   Hume, "David Suzuki."

109   Jonathon Gatehouse, "The nature of David Suzuki," Maclean's, Nov. 18, 2013, *https://www.macleans.ca/society/life/the-nature-of-david-suzuki/.*

110   Janis Ramsay, "David Suzuki zones in on pesticide use during Barrie speaking event," Barrie Advance, April 22, 2016, *https://www.simcoe.com/news-story/6510409-david-suzuki-zones-in-on-pesticide-use-during-barrie-speaking-event/.*

travelling to TV shoots by limousine, rather than ride with the crew.[111] He travels regularly to chill at his pad in Australia.

Yet he rails against airplane travel: "The wealthiest three to five per cent of the world's population are the biggest users of international aviation, while the impacts of climate change fall disproportionately on the world's poorest," he says.[112] A dozen years ago, he promised he would "cut back on flying because it's one of the biggest polluters which causes emission of a lot of greenhouse gases."[113] He said he would only speak to groups outside his Vancouver hometown by video conference, and would give up flying to Australia entirely.[114] "It breaks my heart because I love Australia," he said.

But it didn't really break his heart, because he never gave any of it up. He keeps going back to Australia. He keeps flying around the world. When the Prince Albert II of Monaco Foundation gave him a "Climate Change Award" in 2011,[115] Suzuki was unabashed about using the prize money to fly his wife and kids to French Polynesia.[116] From Vancouver, that's more than 25,000 kilometres round trip. Per person. That's how David Suzuki really lives: By not believing a single word of the anti-oil nonsense that has made him so rich.

---

111   Licia Corbella, "Neil Young chooses his own comfort over his convictions," Calgary Herald, Jan. 23, 2014, *http://www.calgaryherald.com/entertainment/Corbella+Neil+Young+chooses+comfort+over+convictions/9406082/story.html*.

112   David Suzuki, "Airline emissions are flying too high," Rabble.ca, Sept. 14, 2016, *http://rabble.ca/blogs/bloggers/david-suzuki/2016/09/airline-emissions-are-flying-too-high*.

113   Frederick Rocque, "David Suzuki: My Day, My Life," Confidencebound. ca, *https://web.archive.org/web/20080324025054/http://www.confidencebound.ca/content/view/74/31/*.

114   ibid.

115   Prince Albert II of Monaco Foundation, "Award Ceremony, October 7th, 2011," *http://www.fpa2.org/news-299.html*.

116   Ian Bailey, "20 Questions with David Suzuki," The Globe and Mail, Feb. 22, 2018, *https://www.theglobeandmail.com/news/british-columbia/20-questions-with-david-suzuki/article38077211/*.

CONCLUSION:

DAVID SUZUKI IS NO ROLE MODEL

After news of the University of Alberta's plans to honour David Suzuki broke, as outrage and anger swept the U of A campus, the school's faculty, the alumni community, the business community and the province, Suzuki couldn't resist the chance to rub it in everyone's face. He wrote an article about how great it all was, because a "healthy debate about corporate influence over academic institutions and issues around climate-disrupting energy sources has emerged from it," he wrote.[117]

"I'm honoured that the university is giving me an honorary degree for being 'the face of environmental consciousness to generations of Canadians as well as viewers in more than 40 countries worldwide,'" Suzuki humble-bragged in his article, published in the *Calgary Herald*, *The Georgia Straight*, Rabble.ca, on the David Suzuki Foundation

---

117   David Suzuki, "Healthy Debate emerges from honorary-degree controversy," Calgary Herald, May 23, 2018; "Degree sparks necessary debate," The Georgia Straight, May 18, 2018; "Honorary degree sparks necessary debate," Rabble. ca, May 15, 2018; "Degree sparks necessary debate," The David Suzuki Foundation, May 27, 2018.

website, and anywhere else he could find to publish his gloating.[118] "As flattering as it is to be made the fulcrum of debate surrounding fossil fuels, climate change and humanity's future, this isn't about me," he smirked. "After all, what I say about economics, planetary boundaries, and the need to shift priorities is no different than what economists, scientists, philosophers and numerous other experts around the world have been saying for years."

You see, Suzuki is saying, Albertans aren't mad at me. I'm just the scapegoat. I'm just the guy telling it like it is. What Albertans are really mad at, he wants Canadians to think, is science. They're mad at "experts." They're mad at reality. They're in denial. Obviously that's because they love their oil so very, very much that they can't bear to hear anyone tell them they have to give up their precious petro-dollars to heal the planet. And how fortunate the world is that this whole controversy has thrown some much-needed light on that corrupting "corporate influence." And how nice it is to finally talk openly about climate change. Finally! As if Albertans haven't had to endure endless lectures about, and attacks on, these supposedly "climate-disrupting energy sources" for the last 20 years.

Of course, in trying to normalize his own extreme views, Suzuki was lying — again. We've already seen how real scientists — researchers who actually stick to accurate facts and value integrity — have distanced themselves from so much of the junky pseudo-science that Suzuki ceaselessly spews in his mercenary quest for celebrity. But Suzuki pays no mind. He's been caught and called out so many times for his egotistical habit of throwing around dangerous, alarmist lies and misrepresentations just to get his name into the headlines, it's obvious he doesn't actually listen to or care what other experts say. University of Alberta economics professor Andrew Leach, the architect of the Alberta NDP's anti-carbon climate policies, thinks Suzuki has so deliberately and maliciously misrepresented academic research that, "There's no way I'd share a stage with David Suzuki ... not a chance."[119] Mike

---

118   ibid.

119   Tristin Hopper, "Why the architect of Alberta's climate change plan is slamming an honorary degree for David Suzuki," National Post, April 18, 2018

Moffatt, a professor at the University of Western Ontario, has written about Suzuki's actual relationship to these "economists" Suzuki claims in his article are in full agreement with him and have "been saying for years" all the same things he has. Actually, Moffatt says, it's the opposite. Suzuki, he says, "displays a perplexing lack of understanding of basic economic concepts." His comments about economic analysis are "ill informed." Moffatt says Suzuki owes academics "an apology."[120]

Don't hold your breath. Apologizing isn't David Suzuki's style. It doesn't matter if he's caught red-handed peddling his fake science. He refused to apologize when he was caught lying about the nuclear fallout from Fukushima. He refused to apologize when he was caught lying about the alleged disappearance of Great Barrier Reef. Why should he apologize? He's not an actual scientist. He's David Suzuki. He doesn't need to stick to the truth. Facts are for lesser beings. Whatever he says becomes true because he's the one saying it. The words of Canada's "green prophet" are the gospels of Gaia. The man can speak to rivers. What use is there for your mortal "truths" or "science" or "evidence" when you encounter that mystical, ethereal spirit who possesses the magical ability to communicate with water?

The rules for the rest of us never apply to Saint Suzuki. You must sacrifice, he says. You must live in smaller homes, consume less, be colder, hungrier, sicker and poorer. But him? He can have four homes. His primary residence is on a double-sized lot (those single-sized lots can be so crowded, can't they?) overlooking a yacht club, with a gorgeous, unobstructed view of English Bay. It's worth more than the mansions of some celebrities and hedge fund managers. Humans everywhere need to stop procreating because we're spreading on the planet like a cancer, he says. But he can have five kids. He owns a vacation home in Australia, quite literally the other side of the planet — because, why fly a measly three hours from Vancouver to Palm Springs when you can fly five times farther away for a little sand and sunshine?

---

120   Mike Moffatt, "David Suzuki needs an economics refresher course," The Globe and Mail, Oct. 10, 2012, *https://www.theglobeandmail.com/report-on-business/economy/economy-lab/david-suzuki-needs-an-economics-refresher-course/article4602350/*.

You probably work hard and play by the rules. But not Suzuki. He may be a multi-millionaire mega-consumer, but his corporate cash cow claims to be a "charity," so the rest of us end up carrying a bigger burden in paying for the hospitals, schools and the social services that honest Canadians need and value. The David Suzuki Foundation is literally registered with the federal government as a lobbying organization. And it collects funds specifically to fight political battles. Suzuki raised money from the American-based Rockefeller Foundation for "a campaign to support a continuing moratorium on offshore oil and gas exploration."[121] They raised money to "organize" First Nations against Alberta oil projects.[122] Suzuki got paid by the U.K. High Commission to "advance" British policies in Canada – in other words, he took money to promote a foreign government's agenda.[123] Suzuki's group even said it "gladly accepted " money from a video game designer donating the proceeds of the purchase of an eco -terrorist video game where players win by blowing up oil and gas pipelines.[124] His "charity" campaigns in favour of higher taxes on oil and gas companies, in favour of Canada signing UN climate agreements, and of course in favour of more liberal rules for foreign donations to Canadian activist groups like David Suzuki's.[125]

Suzuki has a dozen registered lobbyists in Ottawa and another eight in British Columbia.[126] That's not a charity. That's a political lobby group.

---

121   Vivian Krause, "Suzuki's Funding," Financial Post, April 19, 2012, *http://business.financialpost.com/opinion/vivian-krause-suzukis-funding.*

122   Vivan Krause, "Following the (primarily U.S.) money funding Canada's anti-oil movement," July 2, 2014, *https://www.albertaoilmagazine.com/2014/07/vivian-krause-great-green-trade-barrier/.*

123   "Time to Investigate: David Suzuki Foundation," EthicalOil.org, April 25, 2012, *http://www.ethicaloil.org/news/time-to-investigate-david-suzuki-foundation/.*

124   "Taxpayer-funded pipeline bomb video game sparks controversy," CTV News, March 22, 2013, *https://www.ctvnews.ca/canada/taxpayer-funded-pipeline-bomb-video-game-sparks-controversy-1.1208197.*

125   Letter from Darren J. Reed, JSS Barristers LLP, to Canada Revenue Agency Compliance Division/Charities Directorate, April 24, 2012, *http://www.ethicaloil.org/media/2012/08/2012-04-24-Letter-of-Complaint-CRA-DSF.pdf,*

126   Lobbyist registries.

That's why the Canada Revenue Agency launched an investigation into the David Suzuki Foundation[127] — until a newly elected Liberal government ordered the agency to halt its probe.[128] And yet in 2017, the Suzuki Foundation was able to claim more than $5 million as "receipted donations," meaning they were subsidized by Canadian taxpayers.[129] David Suzuki rails against "corporate influence" but his is a multi-million-dollar, fee-for-hire corporation selling its services and influence to lobby groups, political campaigns and foreign governments. But unlike those oil and gas companies he accuses of corrupting society, he gets to write it all off as "charity."

He clearly doesn't think he needs to follow the government's tax rules, or anyone else's rules, including those of the CBC, the government-funded network that made him a celebrity. The CBC's rules say that its on-air personalities are not allowed to get involved in politics.[130] The rules are pretty strict: even donations are restricted, since a CBC host seen donating to a party or candidate "could have a potential negative impact on CBC/Radio-Canada's impartiality, independence and credibility." It's obvious to anyone, of course, that people who present themselves on a public broadcaster as neutral commentators should not be getting involved in partisan politics on the side.

Well, it's obvious to everyone but David Suzuki. Those are just more rules that don't apply to him. After it came to the light that Peter Mansbridge, host of CBC's newscast *The National*, had been paid to give a speech to the Canadian Association of Petroleum Producers in

---

127   Evan Solomon and Kristen Everson, "7 environmental charities face Canada Revenue Agency audits," CBC, Feb. 6, 2014, *http://www.cbc.ca/news/politics/7-environmental-charities-face-canada-revenue-agency-audits-1.2526330.*

128   Dean Beeby, "Political activity audits of charities suspended by Liberals," CBC News, May 4, 2017, *http://www.cbc.ca/news/politics/canada-revenue-agency-political-activity-diane-lebouthillier-audits-panel-report-suspension-1.4099184.*

129   Canada Revenue Agency, Charities Directorate, "The David Suzuki Foundation," *http://www.cra-arc.gc.ca/ebci/haip/srch/t3010form22quickview-eng.action?&fpe=2017-08-31&b=127756716RR0001.*

130   CBC, Human Resource Policies, "Policy 2.2.17: Political Activity," *http://www.cbc.radio-canada.ca/en/reporting-to-canadians/acts-and-policies/management/human-resources/2-2-17/.*

2012 — even though it had been approved by CBC management and Mansbridge said he has never taken a side on any subject involving the oil industry — the network said it would no longer allow him to do it again.[131]

Yet Suzuki has amassed a personal fortune by working on the side of the anti-oil lobby. Not only that, he has actively campaigned for politicians. He actually appeared in a campaign TV ad endorsing the Ontario Liberals in the 2011 election.[132] He publicly endorsed then Liberal leader Dalton McGuinty in a press release put out by the Liberal party.[133] In 2013, he endorsed a candidate for the federal Liberal leadership, Joyce Murray.[134] Then in 2017, he endorsed a candidate for the federal NDP leadership, Charlie Angus.[135] So basically, if you're a political party running against the Conservatives, David Suzuki is available to offer endorsements for your leadership candidates – but still claim charitable status. Of course, he's also available for any number of other political campaigns: Fighting pipelines, fighting fish farms, supporting Idle No More, supporting the Occupy movement,

131   Paola Loriggio, "Peter Mansbridge defends himself after report of paid speech to oil industry," Feb. 28, 2014, *https://www.thestar.com/news/canada/2014/02/28/ peter_mansbridge_defends_himself_after_report_of_paid_speech_to_oil_industry.html*; "CBC issues new policy for public speaking engagements by journalists," CBC, April 24, 2014, *http://www.cbc.ca/radio/asithappens/friday-israel-suspends-peace-talks-cbc-speakers-fees-ocean-sounds-and-more-1.2903795/cbc-issues-new-policy-for-public-speaking-engagements-by-journalists-1.2903800.*

132   "Liberals pull Suzuki endorsement video from web," National Post, Sept. 20, 2011, *http://nationalpost.com/news/canada/liberals-pull-suzuki-endorsement-video-from-web.*

133   Ontario Liberal Caucus, "David Suzuki: 'I'm offering an endorsement of what Mr. McGuinty has done, absolutely,'" Press Release, July, 21, 2011, *https://www.newswire.ca/news-releases/david-suzuki-im-offering-an-endorsement-of-what-mr-mcguinty-has-done-absolutely-508601731.html.*

134   Aaron Wherry, "David Suzuki endorses Joyce Murray," Maclean's, Feb. 21, 2013, *https://www.macleans.ca/politics/ottawa/david-suzuki-endorses-joyce-murray/.*

135   Elizabeth McSheffrey, "David Suzuki endorses Charlie Angus in race to replace Tom Mulcair," National Observer, Aug. 14, 2017, *https://www. nationalobserver.com/2017/08/14/news/david-suzuki-endorses-charlie-angus-race-replace-tom-mulcair.*

and many, many more[136] — all of them off limits to other charities and CBC personalities, but not to David Suzuki.

In fact, Suzuki not only enriches himself by lobbying for political campaigns while flouting the CBC's rules against it, he's been shaking down the CBC to chip in for his campaigns, too. When David Suzuki held a gala in 2010, honouring himself, for $1,000 a ticket, at the luxurious Four Seasons Hotel (with all the proceeds going to his personal foundation), he made sure the CBC ponied up. "As a partner in David's career, we would like to ask that CBC participate in this celebration by purchasing a table sponsorship at the event," the Suzuki Foundation people wrote in a letter sent personally to the deputy executive director of the CBC.[137] The starting price for a table? $25,000, and up to $100,000. The CBC not only ended up getting a table (it hasn't disclosed which price package), it got talked into paying to become an "official sponsor" and using CBC resources to help promote the Celebrate Suzuki event, too.[138] So, yet more taxpayer dollars to help keep David Suzuki in the luxurious lifestyle to which he's become accustomed.

David Suzuki doesn't just scoff at tax rules and CBC policies. He scoffs at the actual law. He's encouraged protestors to break laws and get arrested in the name of climate action (although he prefers not to get

---

136 Greg Renouf, "Idle No More Unmasked Part I: What Didn't The Suzuki Foundation Disclose In Their Letter To Stephen Harper?" Genuinewitty.com, Jan. 3, 2014, *http://www.genuinewitty.com/2014/01/03/idle-no-more-unmasked-part-i-what-didnt-the-suzuki-foundation-disclose-in-their-letter-to-stephen-harper/*; David Suzuki Foundation, "More than 70 civil society groups across Canada urge halt to pipeline project," May 1, 2018, *https://davidsuzuki.org/press/more-than-70-civil-society-groups-across-canada-urge-halt-to-pipeline-project/*.

137 Letter from David Suzuki Foundation to Bridget Hoffer, Deputy Executive Director, English Communications, CBC, June 30, 2010.

138 CBC Sponsorship Agreement, Sept. 10, 2010, between the Canadian Broadcasting Corporation and The David Suzuki Foundation.

his hands so dirty himself).[139] He's blasted police just for doing their job and arresting trespassers that have tried illegally blocking Kinder Morgan's Trans Mountain pipeline expansion — including Suzuki's grandson, the snowboarding eco-activist Tamo Campos.[140] All this support for this supposed civil disobedience comes from the same man, remember, who wants to lock up politicians just for disagreeing with his environmental policies.

But that's how things should be, according to David Suzuki: One set of rules for us lesser folks and one set of rules just for him, whether they're rules he won't follow about scientific integrity, taxes, criminal behaviour, political campaigning, CBC policies, or the life of carbon deprivation and eco-austerity he says we all must adapt to — except for him.

David Suzuki plainly doesn't even believe it himself when he says about the University of Alberta controversy "this isn't about me." He's just telling another one of his whoppers. And it's obvious. The things he says are not anything like what actual, honest, well-informed "economists, scientists, philosophers and numerous other experts around the world" are saying. Actual academics aren't on Team Suzuki. They reject him. They avoid him. They refuse to be on the same stage as him. And it's for the very same reasons that this controversy also isn't about scientific integrity or healthy debate or academic freedom of speech rights.

As with anything and everything involving David Suzuki, it's all about David Suzuki.

---

139   "David Suzuki and Bill McKibben urge civil disobedience to stop Keystone XL pipeline," Vancouver Observer, June 23, 2011, *https://www.vancouverobserver. com/world/canada/2011/06/23/david-suzuki-and-bill-mckibben-urge-civil-disobedience-stop-keystone-xl.*

140   "David Suzuki blasts RCMP for arresting grandson, Tamo Campos, at B.C. Kinder Morgan pipeline protest," National Post, Nov. 24, 2014, *http://nationalpost. com/news/canada/david-suzuki-blasts-rcmp-for-arresting-grandson-tamo-campos-at-b-c-kinder-morgan-pipeline-protest.*

ACKNOWLEDGEMENTS

Thank you to the Rebel staff for getting this book to print so quickly, to Ben Stanley for his editorial assistance, and to our loyal Rebel viewers.

ABOUT THE REBEL MEDIA

TheRebel.media is a leading independent source of news, opinion and activism. Launched by Ezra Levant and a group of dedicated Rebels after the Sun News Network shutdown, the Rebel is essential for anyone looking for "the other side of the story" in conservative news in Canada and across the world.

For more information about The Rebel, or more copies of this book please go to *www.therebel.media.*

10053655R00039

Manufactured by
Amazon.ca
Bolton, ON